Dedications

For my friend Mei with much Aloha!
R.H.

For Daisy with much Aloha!
Y.G.

ISLAND HERITAGE™
PUBLISHING
A DIVISION OF THE MADDEN CORPORATION

94-411 Kōʻaki Street
Waipahu, Hawaiʻi 96797-2806
Orders: (800) 468-2800
Information: (808) 564-8800
Fax: (808) 564-8877
islandheritage.com

ISBN: 1-61710-280-6
First Edition, First Printing—2015
COP 150508

©2015 Island Heritage Publishing. All rights reserved.
No portion of this book may be reproduced in whole or in part
in any form or by any means without prior written permission
from Island Heritage Publishing. Printed in Hong Kong.

Whale Tales

written by **Ron Hirschi**
illustrated by **Yuko Green**

Pronunciation Guide

Lehua: lay-HOO-ah

Kai: Kye

Koholā: ko-ho-LAH

Megaptera novaeangliae: meg-AP-ter-ah nov-ANG-lee-ah

Moli: mow-lee

Nēnē: nay-nay

Maui: MOW-ee

Note: "ow" rhymes with "cow"

Whale Tales

Aloha Friends of Whales!

Brrrrrr! It's cold in the Alaskan ocean. We've been up here studying humpback whales all summer, and now that it's fall, we're sailing home to Hawai`i.

Captain Mike is skipper of our boat, the S.S. Scoutabout. Auntie Jan is a whale biologist. My brother Kai and I are science helpers. Best of all, our pup Scout is on board too. She spots whales before anybody. Or hears them!

We'll follow the humpbacks on their migration to Hawai`i. Just like us, they're heading for warmer water. But their reason is really special – to have their babies where it isn't so cold!

We'll be whale watching and writing all along the way,

Lehua

Summer Home

Alaska 1

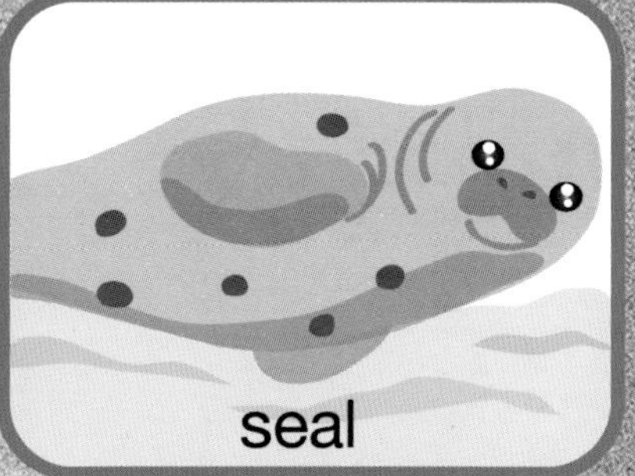

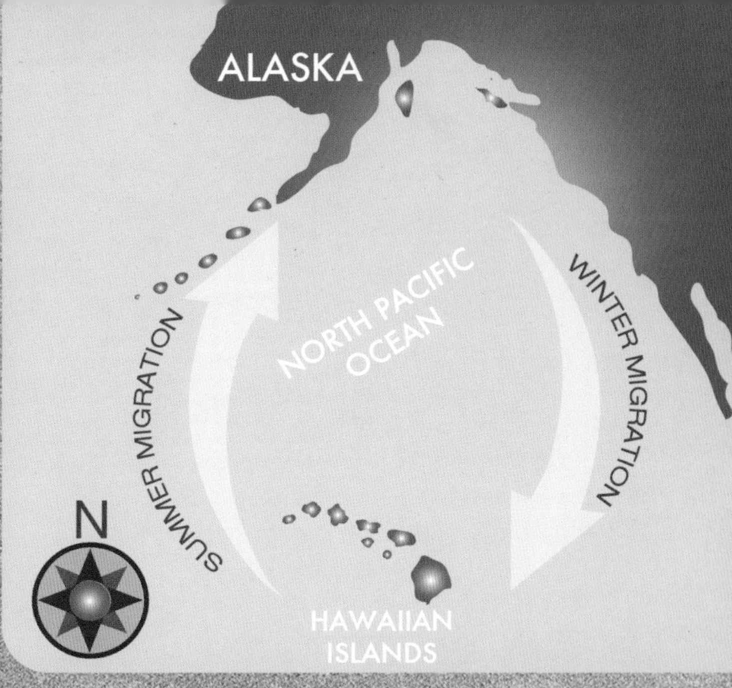

▲ North Pacific Humpback Whale Migration Routes

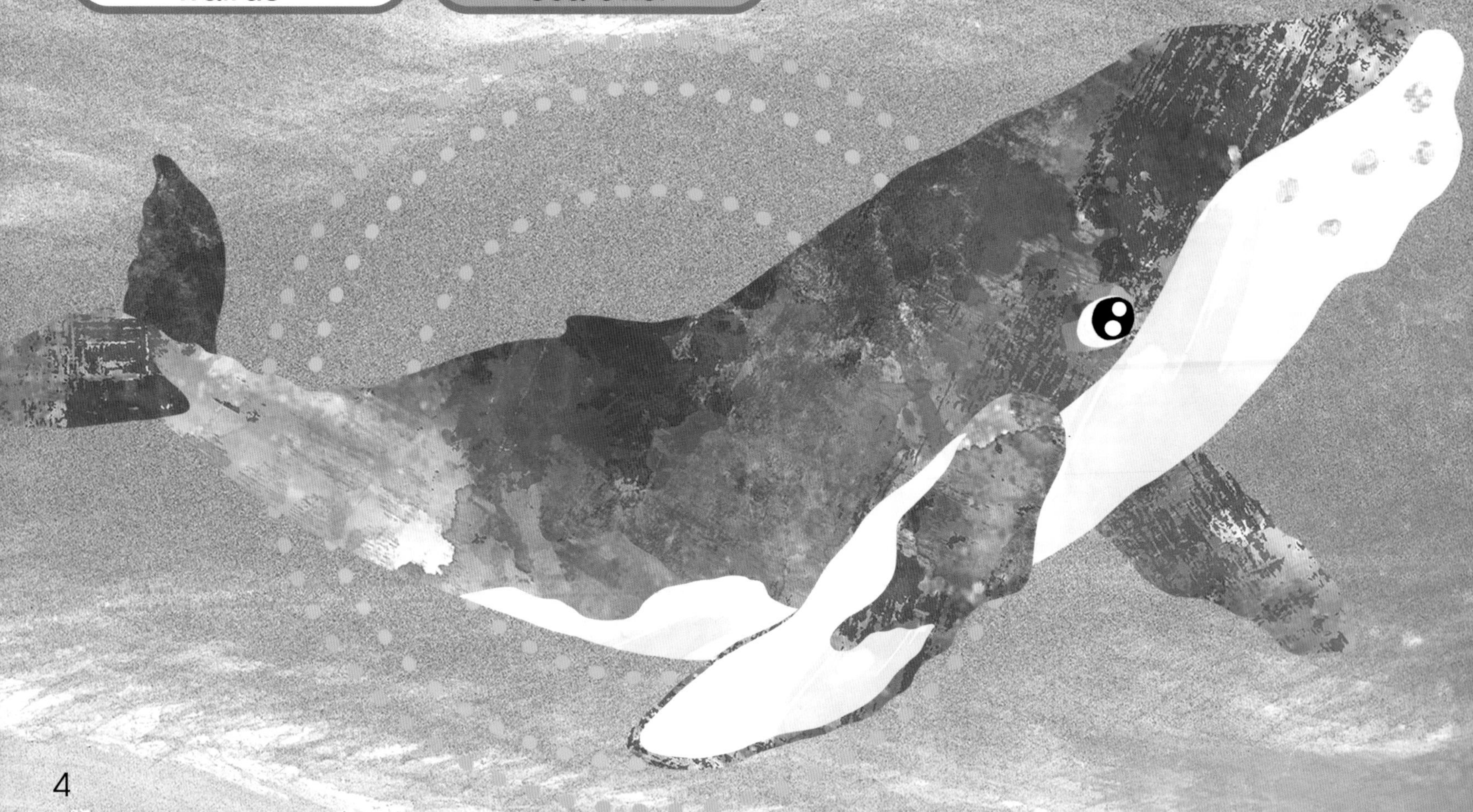

Killer whales, seals, sea lions, and sea otters live in Alaska all year long. Humpback whales are only visitors. They travel a great circle route, swimming nearly 3,000 miles to Hawai`i and back every year.

search site

Alaska is their summertime home. Here they feast on fish and tiny ocean animals like krill that swim in such thick swarms it seems as if the ocean were soup made just for whales.

Whale Scale

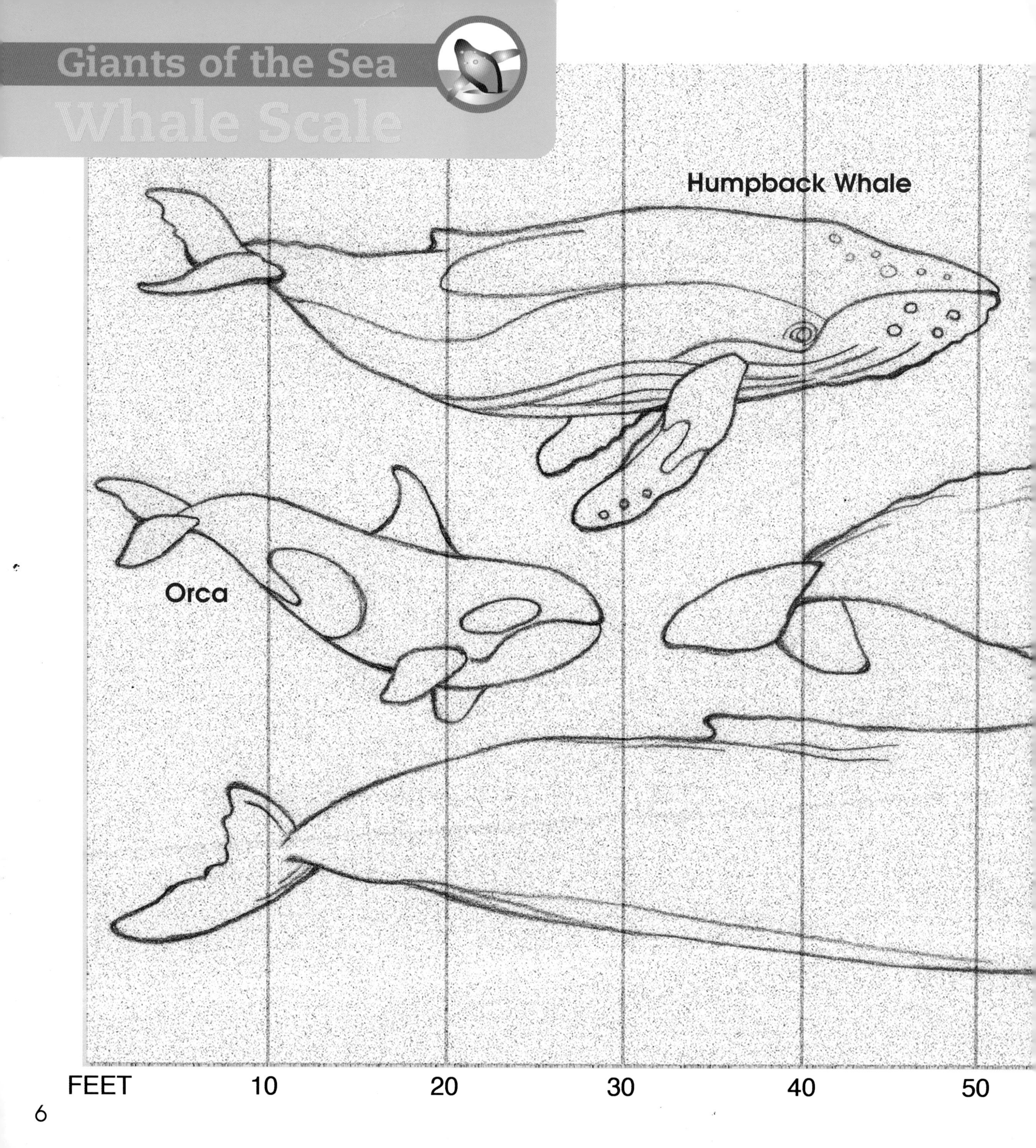

search site

Dear Ocean Friends,

The Scoutabout is 45 feet long, about the same as the biggest humpbacks we saw up close. One day, some killer whales dove under the boat. So awesome to see! The biggest might have been almost 30 feet long. I can't wait to see even bigger whales like the 60-foot sperm whales and the biggest of all, blue whales. Blues can be more than 100 feet, bigger than any creature ever, even dinosaurs!

Aloha, Lehua

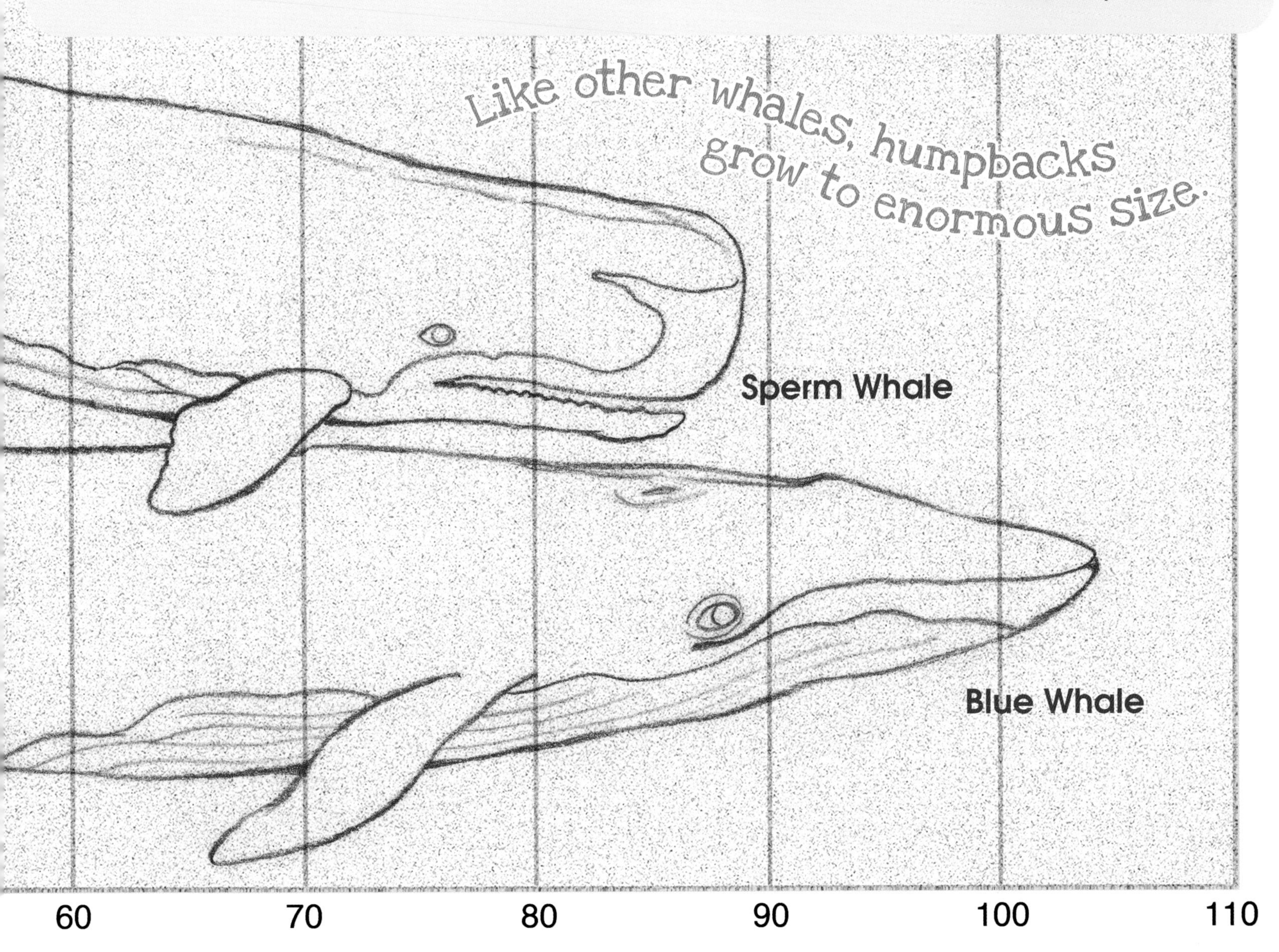

Whale Body 1

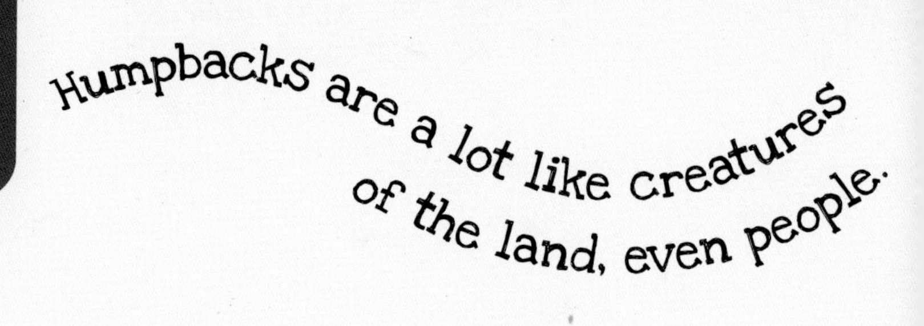

Like all whales, humpbacks are mammals. They breathe air, have warm blood, and even grow hair, though not too much. Like cat whiskers, tiny bristles sprout from bumps on their chin and head. Clumps of barnacles also attach to humpbacks. As many as 1,000 pounds of these hard-shelled sea creatures might grow on just one whale's head. The barnacles thrive in cold, northern waters and don't fare so well in Hawai`i where some or all drop off, to the relief of the whales.

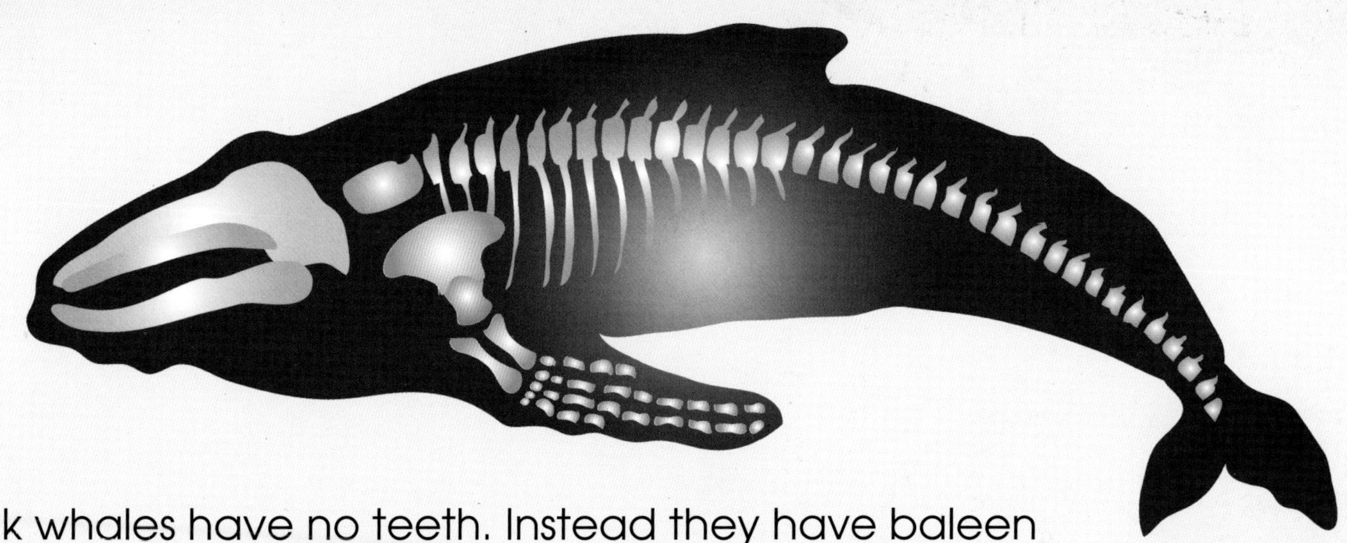

Humpback whales have no teeth. Instead they have baleen that strains small fish, krill, and other food from the water.

Their chin is a huge pleated pouch that stretches to hold a mouthful of food. Their mouth gets even bigger when they pull their tongue back and out of the way – all the way down to their belly button! Once their mouth is full of food - and water - they push their tongue back up to squirt water out the corners of their mouths. The water shoots out as if from a fire hose while the strong baleen strainers trap dinner inside.

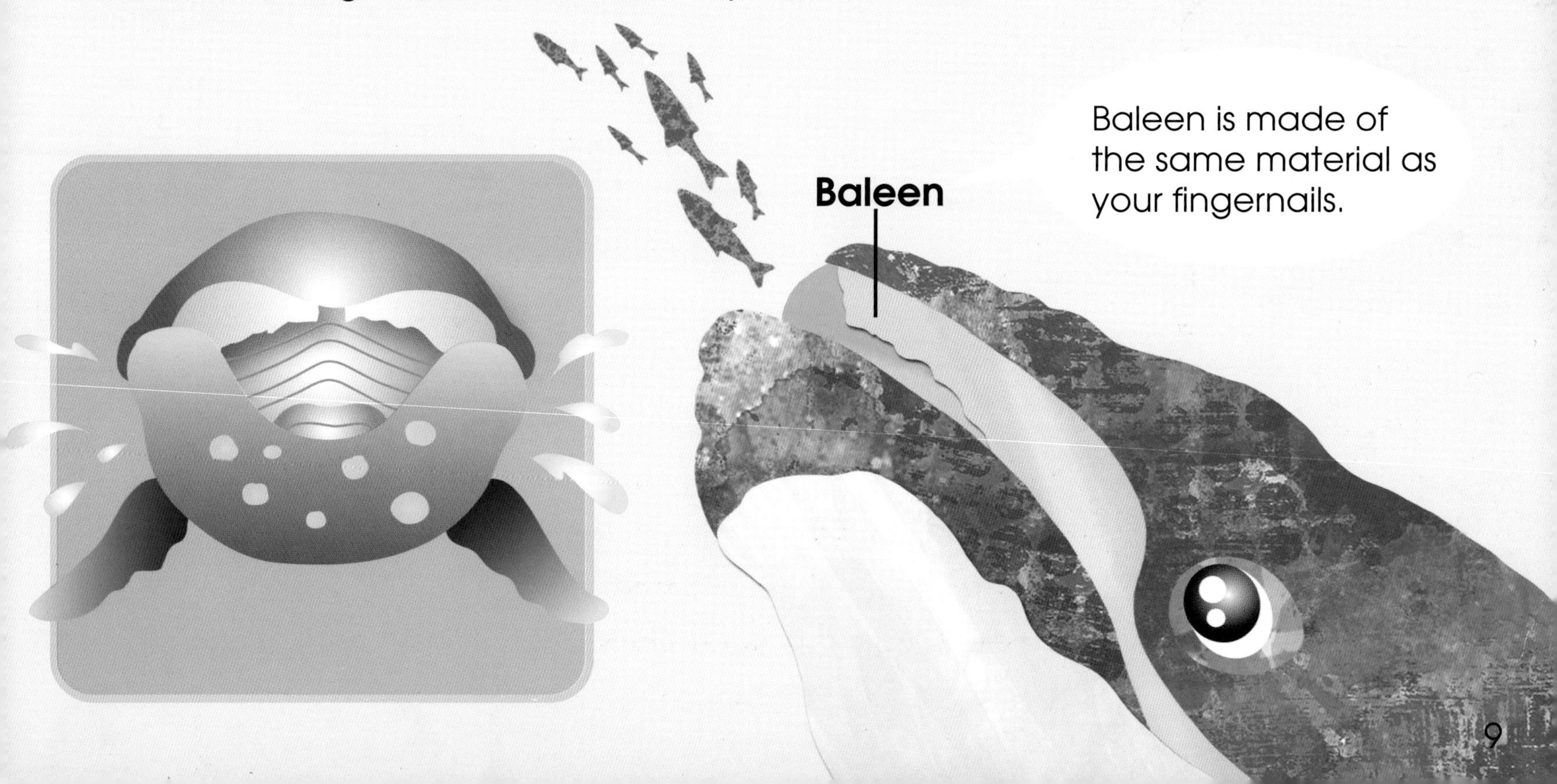

Blowholes

Whale Body 2

Whales dive deep,

Dear Friends of the Whales,

search site

I could watch whales all day! It's so cool to see them spout when they breathe out! Then they kind of pinch their nose – their blowhole – to hold their breath and dive – up to about 600 feet. But deeper divers have them beat by far. Sperm whales can go down for two hours and reach a mile or more in the dark deep to catch giant squid, probably their way favorite food.

Your Friend, Kai the Whale Guy

Giant squid often grow to 65 ft. in length and are very strong.

swim like birds flying beneath the waves,

Humpbacks arch their backs high when they dive, giving them their common name.

Known as *koholā* in Hawaiian, they are also known as *Megaptera novaeangliae*, their scientific name that means, "long-winged New Englander."

The blowholes of baleen whales including humpbacks have two openings.

Did you know?
Whales breathe through their blowholes which are on top of their head. They close their blowholes when they dive.

Feeding Ground
Alaska 2

and eat more than you can imagine.

Humpbacks eat little or nothing at all in Hawai`i and while on migration. A thick layer of blubber is a food reserve that gives them energy during these times. But like a car out of gas, the whales are ready for a fill-up when they return to Alaska. Then they feast day and night.

When humpbacks dine on tiny fish, they often lunge with mouth open wide to swallow as much as a ton of herring, sandlance, or candlefish in one gulp. When feeding on krill, they dive and bob up through thick swirls of the shrimp-like creatures.

Dear Whale Friends,

It's amazing to watch the whales blow bubbles to catch their food. They dive down below schools of little fish. Then they circle together, swimming up to make a huge bubble net that traps the fish. With mouths open wide, the humpbacks scoop tons of fish in just one meal. Puffins and other seabirds are all around, eating the very same little fish. But way fewer for sure.

Catch You Later, Kai

search site

Fingerprints
Whale Tails

No two humpback whales are alike.

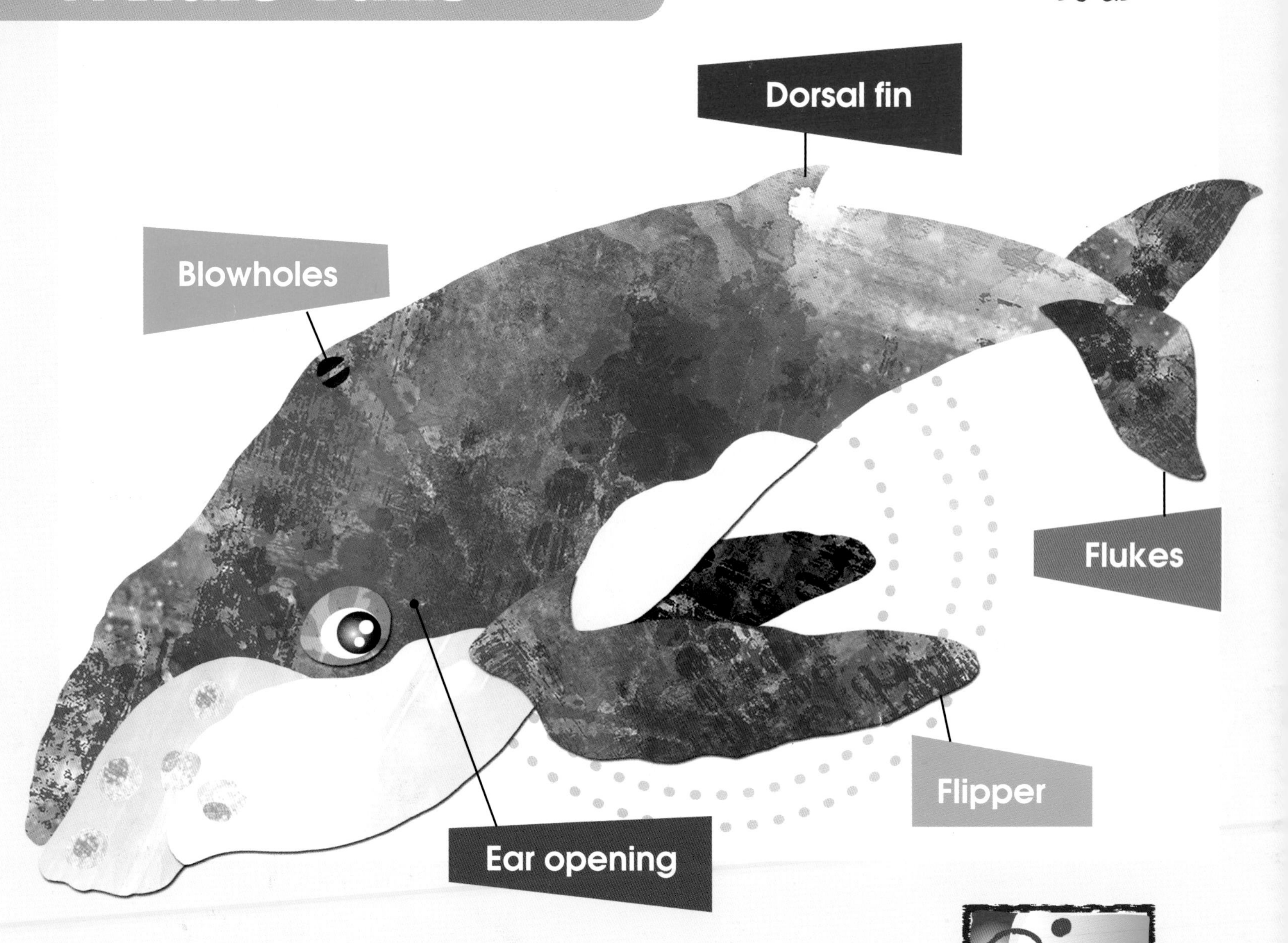

Notches, blotches, and squiggles on humpback tails – also known as flukes – look like abstract paintings. Like lines that make up your fingerprints, these markings can be used to tell one whale from another.

Dear Whale Watchers,

search site

Auntie Jan and I took lots and lots of pictures of whale tails this summer. She sorts the pictures on her computer, giving each whale a number. But Lehua and I give the whales names, and now that we're getting closer and closer to Hawai`i, we're hoping to see some we recognize. I'm especially looking for Barnacle. I listened to her make some interesting sounds but she's a girl, so she doesn't really sing – that's only for the males!

Scientist in Training, Kai

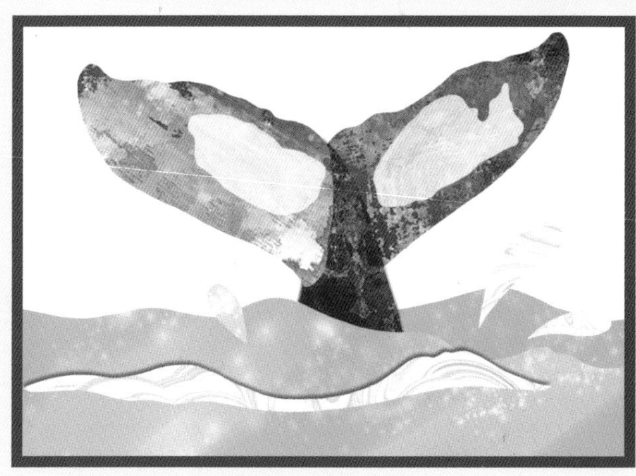

Whale Watch

but all of them splash in mighty leaps and communicate in special ways.

Whales leap free of the waves, splashing as they fall back to the sea. They might leap to help wash barnacles from their skin.

Breaching

They might leap free of the water – called breaching – to help them see into the distance. They might even leap just for fun or to keep in touch with one another.

A smack of the tail or slap with a flipper makes a lot of noise, helping humpbacks communicate. But a crashing, full-body slam by a breaching whale really gets attention.

Waves swoosh and splash. Fish click and shrimp snap. But no sound in the sea is as beautiful as the song of the humpback whale.

Male humpbacks sing just a little in Alaska, as if practicing their songs. But as fall begins, they sing more often, maybe helping one another follow the same migration path. By the time they reach Hawai`i and the breeding season begins, the ocean fills with their schwooooop-bomp-bomp-bomp-schwooooop-bomp-bomp-bomps.....

Hawai'i Bound

search site

Whale Watchers,

Sometimes at night I wonder if the whales are sleeping. Their ocean sparkles from jellyfish and other tiny sea creatures that make light with their bodies.

Daytime, we see our favorite birds - Albatrosses. They soar on seven-foot wings, really close to the boat, kind of like they are in a race with us. Once ashore, we'll be looking for another favorite, the *nēnē*.

Your Friend, Kai

STATE OF HAWAI'I

Northwestern Hawaiian Islands

Main Hawaiian Islands

Pacific Ocean

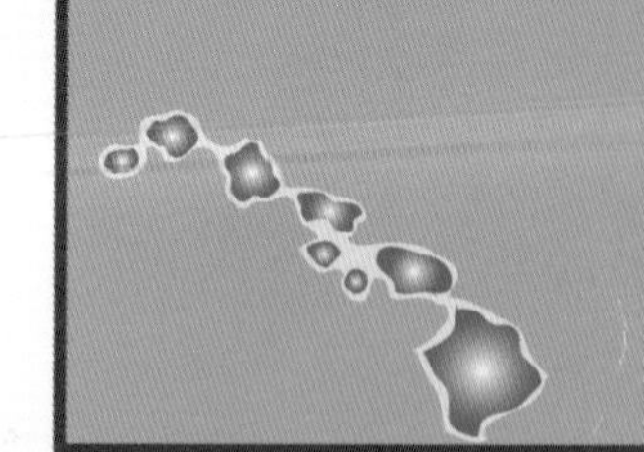

Moli, albatross, spend most of their lives at sea. A favorite food is squid. During winter, most of the birds return to the Northwestern Hawaiian Islands for breeding.

Nēnē, the Hawaiian goose, is the state bird of Hawai`i and an endangered animal.

Whale Comeback

Whale Rescue

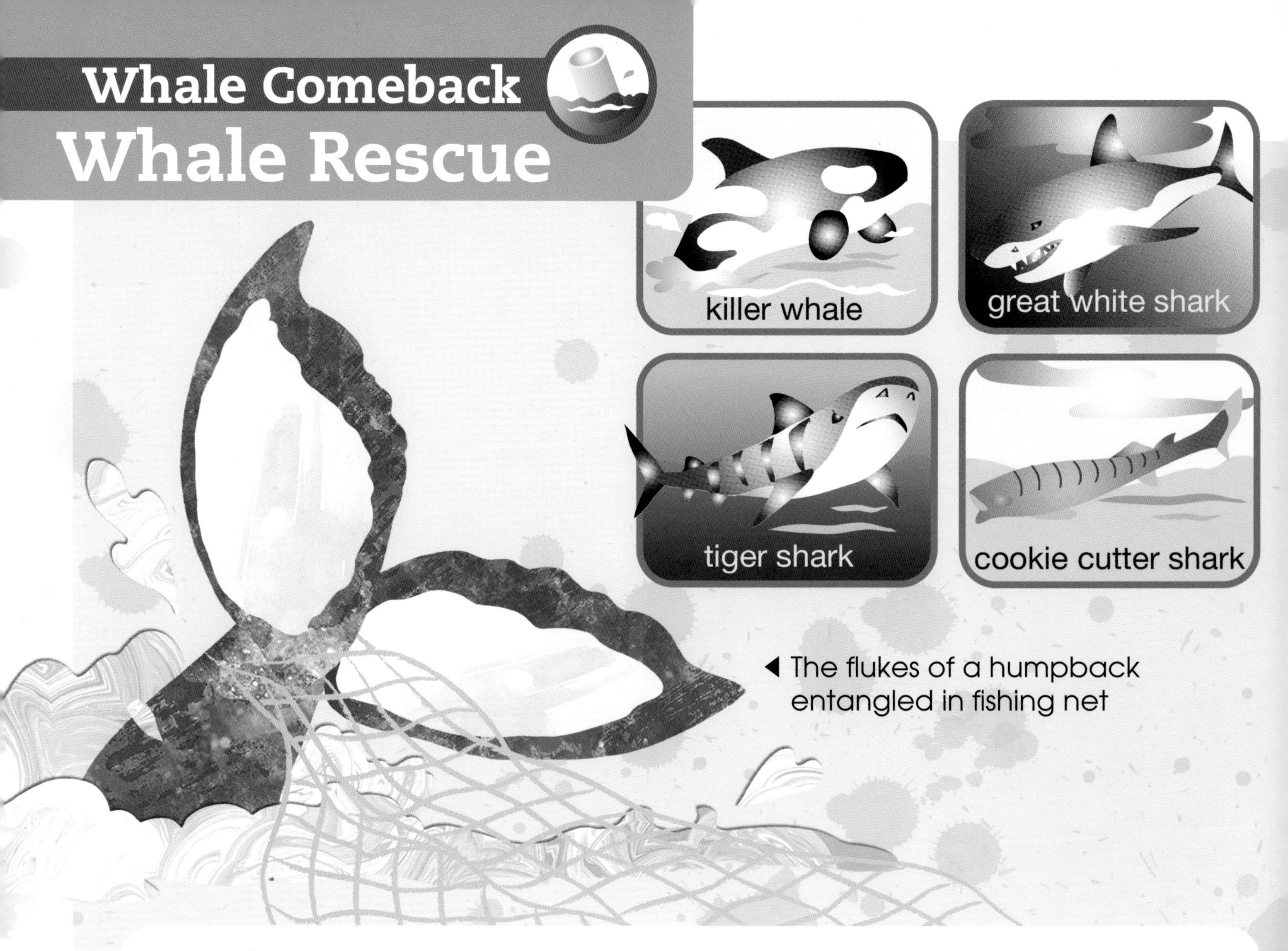

◀ The flukes of a humpback entangled in fishing net

Dear Ocean Friends,

search site

Yuck! Lots of days we see so much trash in the ocean and wonder if the whales are hurt by all this plastic. We try scooping it up, but there is so much it would fill thousands of Scoutabouts. We hear about humpbacks killed when tangled up in trash and nets. They do have natural enemies too – killer whales, great white sharks, tiger sharks, and tiny cookie cutter sharks that leave scars on whale bodies.

Whale Guy, Kai

Humpbacks must be aware of dangers in the sea and keep in close touch with one another.

Dear Ocean Friends,

Captain Mike tells stories of long ago when his Great Grandfather sailed on whaling ships to hunt the humpbacks. Back then, people almost killed ALL the humpbacks on earth. Just for their oil. Hunting was finally stopped about 50 years ago but the whales are still endangered. The good news is humpback numbers are really coming back because people like Captain Mike help them, not hurt them.

Whale Helper Too, Lehua

Whaling ship of the 1800s

Whale Comeback
Whale Song 1

search site

Aloha Whale Friends!

Land and whale songs ho! We can see Maui in the distance and Scout howls to let us know she hears whales singing, especially now that they sing like we never ever heard up north in Alaska.

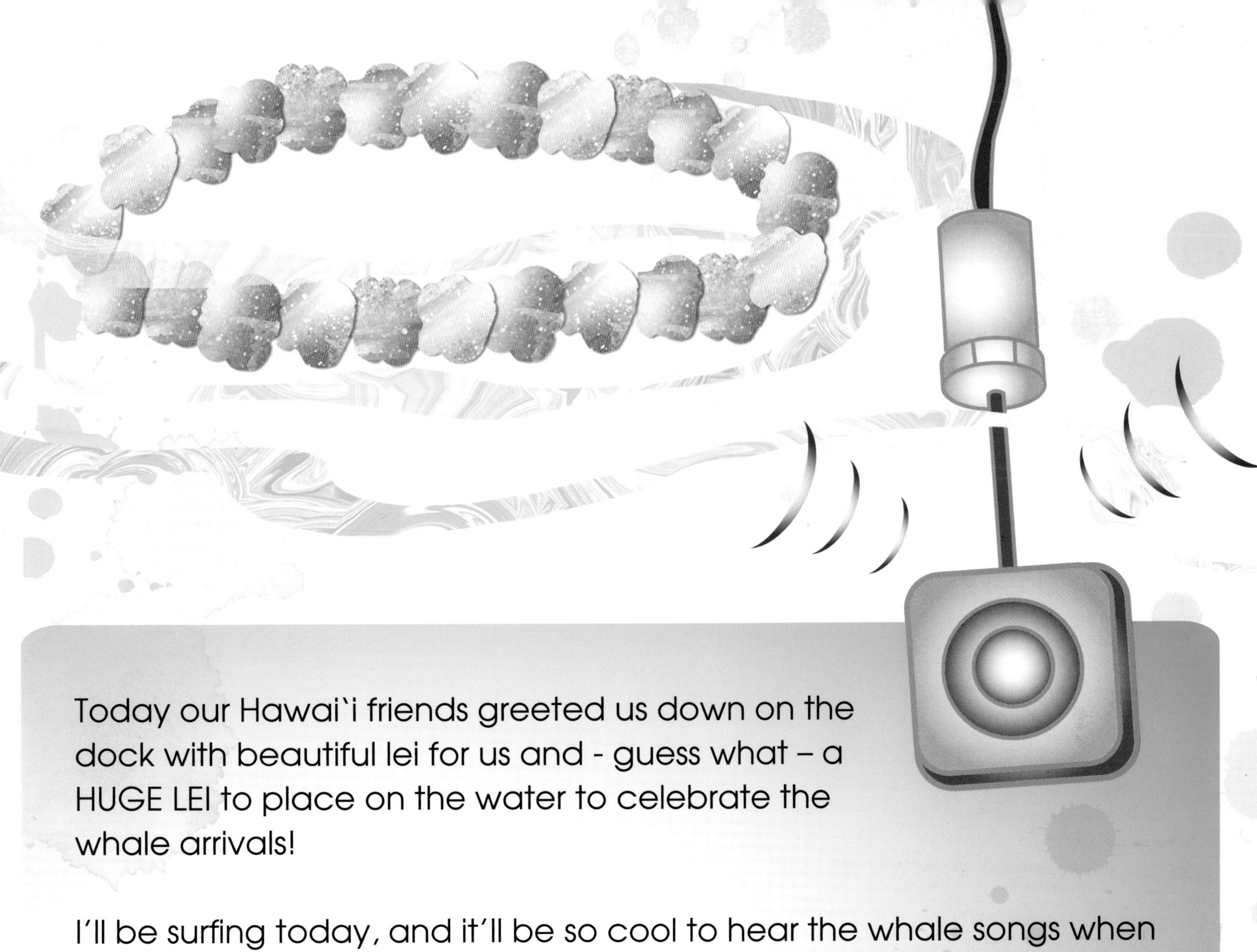

Today our Hawai`i friends greeted us down on the dock with beautiful lei for us and - guess what – a HUGE LEI to place on the water to celebrate the whale arrivals!

I'll be surfing today, and it'll be so cool to hear the whale songs when I am out on the waves.........
Onboard the Scoutabout, we use an underwater microphone to listen to the whale songs. Auntie Jan plays recordings she has made all around the world, and it's fun to listen, since whales sing different songs depending on where they live. That means no other whales sound quite like our *koholā*! Each year they change the songs a lot, and every whale learns the new tunes – to keep in touch.

Surfer Girl, Lehua

Whale Song 2

search site

Friends of the Whales,

It's just the best ever! After surfing and some fun on the beach, we saw our first baby whale today. Some whale moms have their babies along the migration path, but most of them are born here in Hawai`i. But then, just when it all seems calm, the male whales get to singing and even fighting. They butt heads and scratch one another with their big, barnacle-lined flippers.

Auntie Jan says the whales are actually a lot like birds. Like the birds, male whales sing to call attention to themselves. Singing builds a kind of fence around each singer, warning nearby whales to stop short of fighting. Sometimes it works. Sometimes not.....then, it's POW!

Whale Guy, Kai

Male humpbacks fight in the waves during the mating season.

Male whales sing and female whales listen carefully. Singing helps males attract a mate.

A female humpback might pick a male who can sing a long song, proving he can stay underwater for a long, long time. Or she might choose a singing male with a certain special sound. No one knows for sure, and there is much to learn about all the meanings of humpback whale songs.

The Feeding Ground

Whale Nursery

They swim close to their protective mother.

search site

Whale Friends,

Yum! We love being home in the islands and have been eating all our favorites – papaya and some shave ice, too. We catch fish for dinner too. That's fun for us, but it is so strange to think the mom and dad whales won't eat at all until they head back to Alaska next spring. Different story for the babies!

Mom humpbacks are about four to six years old when they have their first babies. Known as calves, the little ones aren't so little. They weigh about 2,000 pounds at birth! And imagine how much milk babies drink every day - more than 100 pounds!!! They nurse for a little less than a year, and during that time, they grow to weigh ten tons. Then calves start to eat fish and live life pretty much on their own.

Aloha, Lehua

A Hui Hou!
Moving On

search site

Whale Friends,

We'll spend the winter helping count whales on each of the Hawaiian Islands. There will be counts once a month to help keep track of where the whales are spending time and how they are doing.

Barnacle's tail looks like this

If you live in Alaska, let us know if you see her there..........She and all the other whales will leave the islands soon, heading back to the north when they must be so very hungry. Maybe we will all sail with them again – up to Alaska, where summer is for whales.

Aloha, Lehua, Kai, Scout, Auntie Jan, and Captain Mike

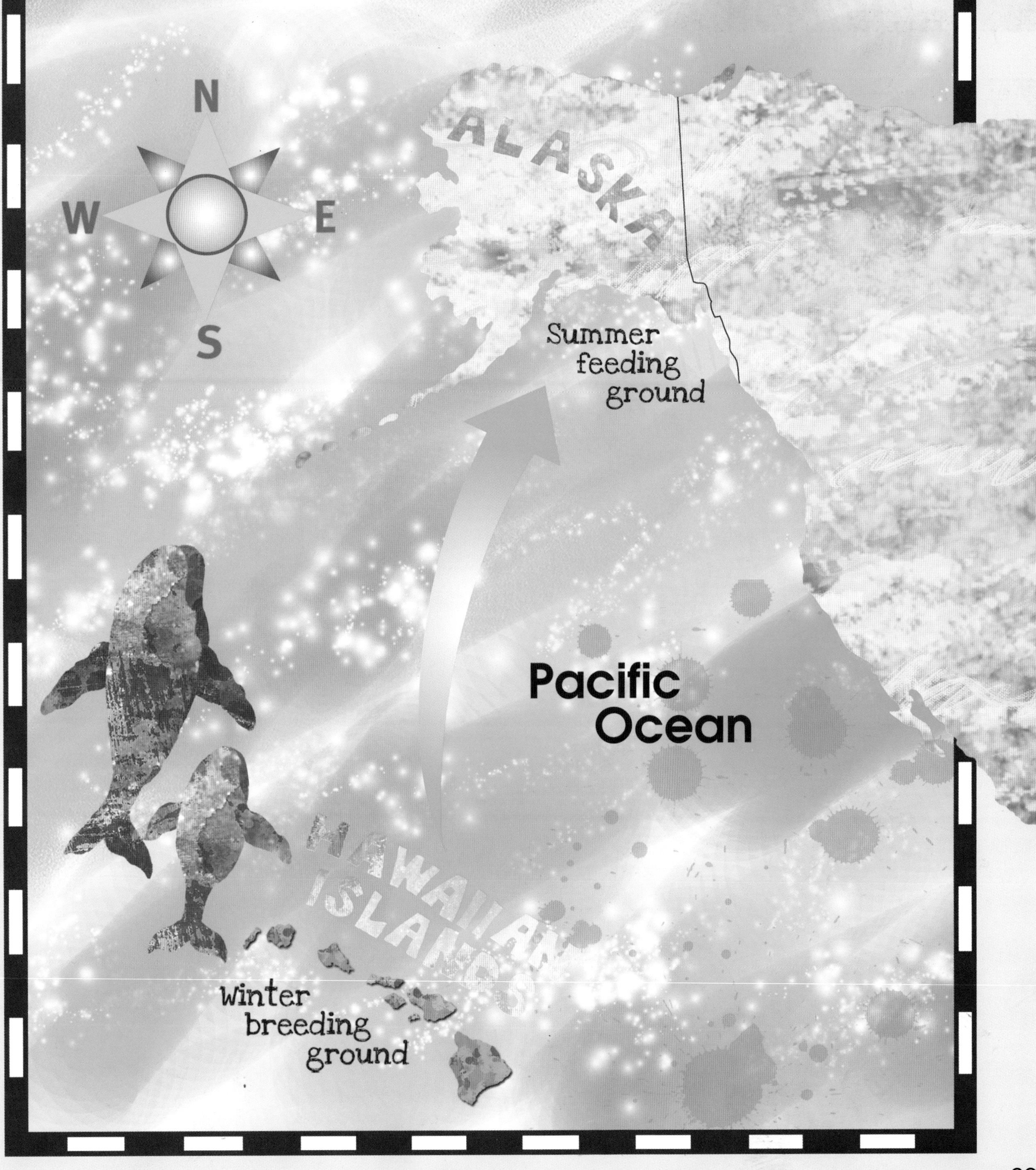
N
W
E
S
ALASKA
Summer feeding ground
Pacific Ocean
HAWAIIAN ISLANDS
Winter breeding ground

Lehua Surfing

Our whale adventure sketchbook

A Hui Hou!

Until we meet again!

About the Author and Illustrator

Ron Hirschi and Yuko Green are both authors and/or illustrators of more than 50 books for young readers, many of which are national award winners. They worked together on Winter is for Whales, a book about Hawaiian seasons. Both are graduates of the University of Washington; Yuko having also graduated with an MA in illustration from Savannah College of Arts and Design.

Yuko teaches high school and has taught art at a K-8 school. She presents workshops in children's book illustration when not creating her own artwork for a variety of products, including greeting cards, stationery, ornaments, puzzles, and toys. Ron has more than 30 years experience as a fisheries biologist and teaches many workshops on ocean ecology. He has led thousands of young people into rivers, streams, ponds and the ocean to study and protect the water world. Recently, he was invited to participate in an environmental leadership project at Midway Atoll in the Northwest Hawaiian Islands. This experience strengthened his belief that the future of the ocean rests in the hands of kids - kids who might learn to love whales so much, they will want to help them.

To learn more about humpbacks in Hawai`i and how to get involved in island whale counts, visit:

http://hawaiihumpbackwhale.noaa.gov